"Your Life"

Scot D. Spooner

authorHOUSE®

AuthorHouse™
1663 Liberty Drive
Bloomington, IN 47403
www.authorhouse.com
Phone: 1-800-839-8640

Published by AuthorHouse 1/23/2012

ISBN: 978-1-4685-3649-2 (e)
ISBN: 978-1-4685-3650-8 (hc)
ISBN: 978-1-4685-3651-5 (sc)

Library of Congress Control Number: 2012900335

Preface

You will soon read about the lifetime and experiences of a common man, who managed to achieve uncommon success. Scot is an inspiration to all who know him, and will soon be a new source of inspiration for those of you that have chosen to read this book. I have no doubt that you will finish this experience with new found inspiration and excitement about getting back to the business of living your life!

I have known Scot for over 25 years, and I know the colorful deck of cards he has often been dealt throughout the years. During the most impressionable years of youth, Scot was subjected to substance abuse, which was soon the catalyst for a broken family and a move from a small farming town to an upper middle class area where we first met. The expected behavior of a teen from a textbook broken family, early alcohol abuse, and being a rough neck thrust into a more affluent area persisted quickly. Due to these circumstances the author found himself in trouble with the law and in the middle of many bad scrapes and confrontations at a very young age. Scot was definitely not known as the "good" kid on campus, nor was he ever nominated for most likely to succeed. Judging Scot on his beginnings, the vast majority of us would come to the valid assumption that his rough and humble start in life was at best average, dysfunctional, and a recipe for a grim future. I speak of his woes not in celebration of such misfortune, nor in bad taste, but to set the stage for what is to follow.

You see I also know the amazing success and achievements Scot has attained in the many years since then. I have always respected people who have risen above the most difficult times in life, rising from the ashes stronger than ever before. This description could be no more fitting than for my friend Scot.

In hindsight, it becomes very apparent that the author's character, success, spirituality and self-confidence could only have been achieved by the difficulties that he experienced and overcame. The pre judged "bad times" were nothing less than blessings in disguise.

Scot's uncommon ability to question convention, what society deems right, or best for its "structure", and the realization that only he and his spirituality can change the final result in the end, is a key ingredient to Scot's success in life. I believe this ideology will also parallel your life, as I am certain it has paralleled mine! After reading *"your life"*, it is quite evident that our lives and how we experience everything in them is governed only by: our perception, things relative to each new set of circumstances, and all of which are influenced by either love or fear.

In closing, I read books of this genre quite often, and I can say with convection that never before have I seen so much experience and wisdom packed into so few pages. Scot's uncanny ability to cut to the heart of so many "issues" that we deal with on a daily basis is nothing less than brilliant. Scot's self-accountability approach for his happiness and success in life is absolutely inspiring. In my opinion, this book will help all of us see that the future is really what we make it, and nothing less.

Adam Dann
Entrepreneur
Longtime Friend

Praise For "Your Life"

Scot succinctly expresses what the Masters of all Ages have known. Your life is not what you do, it is rather how you think and feel about what you experience. We all live lives that outwardly appear to be very different, yet Scot focuses on the not so obvious similarities. A modern day war hero, Scot's life would seem radically dissimilar from yours or mine. When broken down to thoughts and feelings, however, it becomes obvious that our lives are all the same. How we choose to think and feel about what we do shapes our personal experience of life . . . his life, my life, and "your life". Scot shares his unique experiences to demonstrate that we are all one in a world where everything and everyone is connected by the same forces, which shape the human conscience . . . Love and Fear. Scot shows how we can each improve our experience of life by choosing the former, rather than the latter. "Your Life" is a how to manual written by someone who truly gets it! A must read for anyone who desires a more fulfilling experience of the here and now, regardless of what life throws their way.

Ian Goldstein
Trial Attorney

"*Your Life*" is about one man's journey through the ups and downs of his past and how they have shaped his present. Scot uses his own experiences and personal stories to connect with the reader on an extremely emotional level. His book teaches you how to get out of your own way and lead a life of courage, love and faith rather than excuses, fear, and doubt. Reading Scot Spooner's book is like having a life coach at your fingertips and I plan to read it quite often as a reminder of how capable I am of creating a life of happiness and success.

Megan J
Life Coach and Fitness Trainer

"*Your Life*" is a message of love, empowerment and personal responsibility. Mr. Spooner utilizes a retrospective look of lessons learned in his life to impart a positive change in yours. Inspirational and practical, this self-help book fosters your ability to reflect on your past, to evaluate your present and to improve your future. "Your Life" provides a much needed common sense approach to life's challenges that will help you to find focus and clarity in your quest to better your circumstances. It is a must read for those interested in finding improved habits to better negotiate the road of life.

Thanks Scot

Brian B.
Police Officer

At my request, Scot Spooner allowed me to read this book before it was published. I was struggling with understanding the disease of alcoholism and dealing with the disappointment, fear, anger, financial impact and constant worry about my loved one who is an alcoholic. Scot's way of describing reality, provided some clarity to things I had read in other books about recovering from the impact of alcoholism. This book helped me to learn to "surrender" which is something very difficult for a 34 year Marine!

I had immediate confidence in Scot at our first meeting. He is of the "warrior" class. He is a man of direct action and compassion. His courage is evident in his past, and this book. Although he has not told me directly, I know why he is writing this book ... because it is our lives ... and he wants to help us.

Major General Jerry Humble, USMC (Ret)
Public Speaker and Entrepreneur

I've learned that people act within, and react to the circumstance of life differently. It's dispiriting to discover how many are unprepared and unwilling to figure out their path through life, or never truly explore the mystery that is their life. Hope in the human condition prevails when I meet people who "Get it." Scot Spooner is a man that "gets it."

When I was bestowed with the lessons of *"your life"* and allowed to peer a little deeper in Scot's assessment on his life, my life, your life. I learned that we all want the same things, share the same fears, and have the same needs. The only difference is how we perceive life, and how we translate our experiences.

This book is "My Life," from a different vantage point.

Nathan Noble
Small Business Owner and Entrepreneur

My Inadequate Thanks

The thanks that I want to give in these next few paragraphs will not adequately convey the total amount of gratitude that I feel for those I want to recognize. I know that the only true measure of thanks worth giving will come in a lifetime of actions not words, which I plan to take in order to show my thanks and appreciation to these amazing people.

I would not be here, much less have the courage to write this book, were it not for my relationship with a God that I have come to know, love and depend upon, and I would not have this special relationship with my God, if not for the unconditional love and loyalty of my wife Stacy. Although I have listed God first and Stacy second, it was my relationship with my wife that enabled me to seek my own truth in life, and in doing so, find my personal relationship with God. You are beautiful in every way Stacy. Thanks for never giving up on us or me, even when I had given up on both. I love you!

To those who have always been there,

Tom Spooner, David Spooner, Adam Dann, Ian Goldstein, Blake Horst, James Houston, Bobby Parker, Richard Casey, Jasper Davis, Jim Spratt and Gregg Scott; you all have been a huge part of my story, and of my personal journey through life. Thank you for your support, but more so for your friendship. You are all truly amazing men, and I am blessed to have you in my life.

To Chloe and Jake,

You are the most amazing kids that a dad could ever wish for. I am truly blessed to have you in my life. I love you both more than words can ever say. I'll never forget what you said to me the night I told you I was going to write this book: "Your book will be a best seller dad" (Chloe Spooner). You were right baby! Thank you Bears!

To Mom and Dad,

For your unconditional love and support, I will always be grateful; for I know that there are many that will never be able to say the same of their parents, which makes me one of the lucky ones. Thank you both.

Introduction

So how is it that you are picking up a book written by someone who obviously knows nothing about you yet is so presumptuous as to imply that you will soon be reading about your life?

That's a valid question, and one that I will do my best to answer.

This book is primarily about my life, but I hope to show you that my life is nothing more or less than your life from a different perspective.

This may seem an extreme oversimplification of what appears to be play on words and hard to believe, but I believe it to be true.

We may all look different, think differently, come from different places, speak different languages, and have our own opinions, but the things we differ on pale in comparison to the desires, problems, and needs that we share. For at the core of all of our complexities lie very simplistic truths, should we have the desire and courage to look at them.

I have wanted to write this book for several years but didn't feel that I had all of the material necessary until this very day, this very moment—9 a.m. EST, June 6, 2011, my own personal D-Day.

I am no different from any one of you who is reading this. I will never claim to have the capability to personally help any of you achieve anything, but what I can do is present my life lessons to you so that you may in turn decide to make positive change happen in your life. My hope is to be a good messenger. What you do with the message is up to you.

I believe that my life experiences and lessons learned have the power to help you achieve whatever you desire, should you possess the strength and courage necessary to take full responsibility for your life's circumstances. If I were to sum up the theme of the content that will follow, it would require two words: personal responsibility.

Dedication

The key inspirations that facilitated the complete transformation of the man that I was into the man that many (myself included) thought that I could never become, are no less than eight of the greatest authors and teachers that I have ever experienced. Please notice that I used the word *experienced*, not *read*. This is because these authors did not merely write words; they supplied me with knowledge and tools that were meant to be taken from the written word, into the mind as concepts, and through the trials of applied effort, which in turn supplied me much more than quiet afternoons with good books. They provided me with a new lease on life. Their written words supplied me with a blueprint of my own making to be edited and executed in a format and design that is mine and mine alone.

These special people are listed below in the order that I remember their influence on me, with no insinuation regarding the amount of impact that each had on me, for each had its place and entered my life at the perfect time, just as I believe this book has entered your life at the perfect time:

- Dr. Bob
- Bill Wilson
- Emmitt Foxx
- M. Scott Peck
- Wayne Dyer
- Seth Godin
- Dale Carnegie
- Neale Donald Walsch

Although many authors have had an influence on my life, these produced works of art that I have read, underlined, highlighted, talked about, and reread many, many, many times.

It is my hope that these inspiring authors come to someday know how their life's work and advocacy of seeking the truth for oneself have inspired me to live life in the manner that it was designed to be lived—free.

Bottom Line Up Front

O f the many acronyms that I learned in my seventeen years in the US Army, BLUF is one that has applications in all aspects of life. It is simple and requests the same: Give it to me straight, and let's not waste any time getting there.

That being said, if you are a person who is at a point in your personal journey where you have reached total contentment in each and every aspect of your life, you may want to spend your time doing something else because, if this is the case, you absolutely need to be writing a book, not reading one!

For those of you who are still reading, allow me to let you in on the highlights of what the following pages will have to offer.

It is my intention to share with each of you how it is that I have become successful, happy, healthy, and comfortable in spite of many "unfortunate" circumstances and, moreover, my many flaws, lack of formal education, huge fears, and character defects.

I believe that an entire book could be written, or has been written, on each of the ideas found in this book, but I believe your time will be best served by quickly examining what I believe to be these truths or lessons as they apply to life and how each lesson or truth influenced my life.

I am not a formally trained writer; I do not possess a PhD in anything or a four-year degree from an institution of higher learning. I am a high school graduate and just barely pulled that one off.

So what, then, shall I tell you that this book is grounded in if not in formal education? Simply put, I have a self-appointed PhD in life expierience, which I believe more than qualifies me to write this book.

In a nutshell, I hope to pass on to you the truth as I have come to know it, hoping that you will choose to learn from it and move from where you are now to a place you think you cannot go or rise to a level that you think cannot be achieved.

By the way, the fact that over one million people are now reading this book is proof enough that anything is possible!

Thank you for the amazing support!

Now for an extremely important point that I need to make: nothing that I will convey in this book is truly "mine" or even close to 100 percent original. Behind all of the lessons, truths, and opinions that I will share with you are thoughts, words, and lessons that come directly from those whose shoulders I stand upon and are nothing more than their concepts and ideas from a different perspective.

Why is it that the same material continues to be re-created and rewritten over the years? I am not exactly sure, but the time I spent as a teacher taught me that no two students learn the same way. On some days, I would have to teach the same material over and over, and with each small detail change, another student would catch on. I was saying the same thing, just using a different analogy, switching a few words, or maybe drawing a picture. All of this effort was necessary if everyone was to learn the material I was teaching. I find life in the "real" world to be no different than that in the classroom, so the real goal here is to reach those of you who did not understand these concepts, truths, and lessons when they were presented to you by another author or teacher.

IV
Starting with the "Why"

From the day we are old enough to speak until the day we die, we insistently use this word in our endless search for the meaning of all things in life. Our need to understand starts with the same word over and over again: Why?

So why is it so important to ask the question, and why is it so imperative that we get the answer? It's simple—it provides comfort and direction through the knowledge we gain as a result. The scariest situation for us humans to be in is one in which we don't have all the information. We have to know why before we can move forward.

Knowing the "why" provides the closure we need in many circumstances. It provides the direction required to move forward or the information needed to stop doing something.

Then there are times that the exact opposite will happen. As children, we always ask why, but as adults, there are many times that we are scared to ask why because to do so would shed light on a subject that we would have to research and study, bring out the truth that we fear, or, worst of all, require work or change on our part. So most times we choose to sit silently, maintaining the status quo, making no waves, and settling for less than we could have or should have achieved.

I think it is important that you understand why I chose to write this book and why I think that its contents are important enough for you to read.

I chose to write this book because I have come to believe that anything is possible for any person, and I mean anything. This does not apply just to me, nor is there a magic fairy that sprinkles pixie dust on a few selected humans who get to become happy, healthy, wealthy and content. This is for all who inhabit the earth—a bold statement, I know, but one that I believe to be true.

I want a life of abundance and wealth for all who read this book, and for all in the world, for that matter, and I have chosen to believe it is possible. Otherwise, why bother writing the book?

Now for the more important question: What enables me to think that I personally possess the wisdom that will help you achieve greatness in your life? To answer that completely, I will have to tell you about where I have been, where I am, and where I am going.

My story should quickly demonstrate why it is that I believe that you are reading about portions of, if not all of, *your* life. Why? You might ask. It's because I am an average human who came from very little, suffered through plenty, made many horrible decisions, and in spite of myself, achieved things that should have been impossible according to many.

I come from a mid- to lower-income family and was raised in a rural farm town. I want to point out that if that first sentence had read, "I was born with the proverbial silver spoon in my mouth," it really would not make a difference. I believe that those born into riches often suffer more than those who go without. OK, back to my life with the wooden spoon.

I was born in the same hospital as Mel Tillis, for you old country music fans. I have a brother who is five years my senior and a sister who is six years my junior. Yes, I had a full case of "middle child syndrome," and, damn it, it is a real condition! ;)

I have an alcoholic father, and my parents divorced when I was twelve. I was a full-blown alcoholic with a pack-a-day habit by age fourteen.

I was arrested for the first time at age thirteen and again at seventeen just prior to joining the army. Once I joined, I never looked back. I served in the army for the next seventeen years and went to combat several times. After I got out of the army, I joined a start-up company and was fired eighteen months later.

So let's recap the highlights, or in this case, the "lowlights": I had an alcoholic dad, and I am an alcoholic. I come from a broken home, was in handcuffs a couple of times before I was eighteen, served in combat, suffer from Post-Traumatic Stress Disorder and about five other multi-letter afflictions, do not have a four-year degree, failed at my first business venture, and will forever be scarred by middle child syndrome. Whew! I need some kind of anonymous meeting after reading that.

So based on that picture, you are reading a book written by a guy who should, for all intents and purposes, be something between an absolute failure and a guy on the rocks, at best. But I am pleased to tell you that I am far from either. Now to a few of the highlights.

By the time I was eighteen, I was an infantryman and US Paratrooper in the 82nd Airborne Division—more commonly referred to as "The Division" by those of us in "the biz." After spending a few years in the 82nd, I decided to have a run at Special Forces, and at the ripe old age of twenty-two, I was awarded the Green Beret, which I wore proudly for the next fourteen years. During my time on a Special Forces Operational Detachment Alpha, I traveled the globe, training, jumping out of planes, shooting guns, and blowing stuff up.

During this time, I was reunited with the long lost love of my life, Stacy, and was married three months later. Shortly thereafter, I became the father of a beautiful daughter, Chloe.

My beautiful girls and me!

After having a successful run in 3rd Special Forces Group (Airborne), I was assigned to the John F. Kennedy Special Warfare Center and School to become an explosives instructor. When that tour ended, I chose to be assessed yet again for the most elite unit that the US Army had to offer and was accepted. I was assigned to the First Special Forces Operational Detachment Delta for the remainder of my career.

My last six years in the military proved to be quite a culmination event and an amazing opportunity for me to put into practice my many years of training and leadership experience. During this time, I would face every fear one human can experience, feel the exhilaration of a roller-coaster ride, and cry bitter tears over the loss of many friends. During those six years, I also became a father yet again, this time to my "man cub," Jake.

I feel certain that these years were the fire necessary to mold me into the man, husband, father, and leader that I am today.

The previous few paragraphs were not written in any attempt to toot my own horn, only to make a point of the success that came from a guy who was not set up for success, making each victory a big deal for me and for those who thought these achievements impossible for a guy like me.

Allow me to back up for a moment to make a point that I believe is necessary in painting this picture. After seventeen years in the army—a short three years away from lifelong retirement checks and health benefits—I made a decision that rocked the foundations of all who knew me.

I left the army, turned down my promotion to Sergeant Major, and jumped headfirst into the wild world of a start-up company. I decided to go with my gut, go after my dreams, and make my first million. A short eighteen months later, I got a call from my CEO that would forever change my life. For the first time, I was fired. It was a moment that I will never forget. You see, I had never failed to achieve what I set my mind to do, nor did I believe it to be possible.

My stomach churned, tears welled up, and I thought, *Look what you have done to your family.* I felt anger, rage, shame, regret, and remorse. Little did I know then that this experience had to happen. That's correct—it had to happen.

It is always darkest before the dawn.

So that takes us to the present day and the most exciting time in my life. I am for the first time truly free of all outside influences and outside direction, and I am the captain of my ship. I have an extremely scared wife, a big mortgage payment, no pension plan, no salary, no benefits, and no guarantees—just life experience, a desire to win, and the faith to see it all turn into the success story worthy of my second book.

The final reason I wanted to write this book was to convey as much experience into as few pages as necessary. I have read many books, listened to many speakers, and had many conversations with wise individuals. I have always thought, *Wouldn't it be great if I could take all of that information, lessons, and truths and put it all in one place so that people could gain a ton of insight with only a small investment of time?* So that is what I have done my best to do.

What follows will be a recipe for living a great life that has worked out well for me. There are many "recipes" out there that will work as well as, if not better than, mine, so please know that I know my way is not the only way. It's just one of many, and it can work for you too.

Let's get started by getting into what I believe will change your life should you choose to learn from these ideas, truths, and lessons and take full responsibility for "Your Life."

By the way, my dad has been sober since 1987, and I have been sober since 2002. My dad is an absolute role model for me, and I am forever grateful for his friendship and love, which he has graciously given through the years even as he sat silent, watching me burn my life to the ground.

There is always hope for those who seek the truth, face the facts, and do the work.

Table of Contents

Chapter One

Terminal Uniqueness

An illness that I suffered with for many years is one I refer to as terminal uniqueness. Please notice that I used the word *with*, not *from*. This is because it was an illness that I chose. I use the word *terminal* because this illness is nothing less than the equivalent of any stage four disease that can last for decades, or a lifetime.

What does terminal uniqueness sound like? What does terminal uniqueness look like?

Here are some examples of what it may sound like:

- "You don't know what life is like for me."
- "If you had to deal with my life, you would be this way too."
- "That may work out great for you but not for me."
- I'm too *<fill in the blank>* to be able to do that."
- "You don't know what I have been through."
- "I had a terrible childhood."

The list could go on for pages and pages, but I am sure you get the point.

Terminal uniqueness looks like any one of us, and it looked just like me for many years.

I have used every one of those lines at some point in my life, but I no longer allow myself to do so. It doesn't mean that I don't have those thoughts run through my mind. I have bad days just the same as you. The difference is that I choose not to speak them, empower them, or act on them.

Please know that I do not make light of any of the situations that you may have gone through in your life. Horrible experiences are real, and the pain is real. What I want to point out is that working through the pain and suffering is one thing, but to be defined by it is another. It is my hope that you will never be defined by the wrongs done to you but that you will be defined by the positive way you choose to live your life—here, now, in the present moment only.

The truth that I have come to find for myself is that I am not unique. For each and every situation I have lived through, many others have too. It became a personal obsession in my life to find those who had lived through these same "not so unique" experiences and uncover the secret to coming out on the other side stronger, and doing so with dignity. I added the phrase "doing so with dignity" because there is a big difference between getting through something by kicking, screaming, blaming, and yelling versus keeping calm, taking responsibility, and having faith. Getting through hard times and not owing anyone an apology once all is said and done is what I am speaking of.

It is in the seeking that I find the answers, yet that alone has afforded me nothing in the way of change. It takes knowledge followed by action and faith to "get to" where the others are currently, which is where I *said* that I wanted to be. Right? Right!

The other nugget of wisdom that comes with seeking out those who have suffered as I have is that I quickly find that many people have stories that make my story look like a walk in the park. This turns my complaints into gratitude and hope, both of which are priceless.

I am not unique (even though my mom still tells me I am), and you are not unique, which is yet another reason that this is "your life" written by me.

Seek the answers, face the facts, make a plan, and execute with the faith and hope necessary to succeed. Remember, your life is a fairy tale to many of the suffering people in this world.

Chapter Two

A Degree from Barnes and Noble

Some years ago, I began to do my best to seek out and surround myself with what I believed to be successful people. Each person had his or her own story and own level of success, so I played close attention to all of the details, in search of as many similarities as I could find.

The one common thread that could not be argued was that all were avid readers. That is the first part. The second and more important finding about their reading habits is that none of them read fiction materials, or if they did, it represented 2 to 5 percent of their libraries. Another similarity is that they watched very little television and definitely no reality shows. No judgment here—I'm just saying.

I made myself a promise that I too would read the authors who were placing lifetimes of knowledge into a couple hundred pages, and I would not just read them but would look at each as if it were a textbook for life. I was told this great analogy years ago, and I want to share it with you: If you come eat apple pie at my house and find that it is the best apple pie that you have ever had, you will ask me for the recipe, and I will give it to you. You could then easily go to the store, buy the ingredients, and cook the exact same pie. But if you added anything or took anything away, you would not end up with the best pie in the world, which you have the recipe for.

I bring this up to make a point about the importance of following directions. When I pick up a book to learn how to do something or I ask someone advice on how they achieved a certain task, I always have three options of what to execute after I gain the knowledge that the person or the book has provided:

1. I can take the recipe, which was successful, and execute the exact same plan.
2. I can use some of the person's plan mixed with some of my plan.
3. I can use none of the person's plan.

More often than not, the best way to achieve the task in question is to use the plan that has worked. This was a hard lesson for me to learn, but the older I get, the more I find that reinventing the wheel is not a great plan! After I go to a source for answers, it is in my best interest to at least start out with the blueprint that has already worked and make small adjustments as I go.

Here are some of the many nagging questions that I used to carry around in my head:

- Is there more to life than this?
- When will things change for the better?
- Isn't there an easier way?
- Can dreams come true for a person like me?
- Why am I walking around so angry?
- Why am I so scared?
- How come I am in turmoil with so many people?

- How come I am never satisfied?
- How come that idiot is rich and I'm not?

As will be the *modus operandi* with all of the lists that follow, it could go on for page after page and each of us would be asking different questions. The problem is that none of these questions are answered in common textbooks. The required information can be thoroughly researched only by finding those people who have answered these questions for themselves. In my first attempt, I did the next best common-sense thing: I went to the book store and started building my research library.

I love to share knowledge with people, so after I would read a great book, I would give it away in hopes that the recipient too could gain some insight from the material. The lesson that I learned from this behavior is twofold: if a book I buy is worth finishing, it is worth keeping as a research book; and second, we are able to receive a message only when we are ready, and when that time comes, we take action.

You see, it takes effort to get in your car, spend your money, and obtain a book that someone recommends, and this effort is the first step to gaining the knowledge held within those pages. My giving books away did very little for those I gave them to, for they had to put no effort into gaining the knowledge, which usually meant that it was simply a kind gesture to them and a trip back to the bookstore for me, plus more money from my wallet spent on the same book for the second and third time. So I have made it a rule to only suggest books, not give them away. I do make exceptions in extenuating circumstances, but they are rare.

My thirst for knowledge in answering all of the questions that I pondered had begun, and it continues to this very day. It is my intention to never quench the thirst for knowledge that is rooted deeply in my soul.

Your questions may be exactly the same as mine, or they may be totally different, and that is OK because between all the bookstores and the Internet, you will find the answers you seek once you decide to do the legwork.

I could go on and on about all of the books that I have read, but that would not be the most efficient use of either of our time. I will be referencing many of them as I continue to write; as I said before, this was all someone else's material before it was mine.

I encourage you to write your list of questions and become devoted to the effort required to read the books or have the conversations that will give you the education that few choose to attain. Go ahead. I dare you!

Chapter Three

Unlearning Years of False Truths

Before you read the next sentence, please humor me and close your eyes, clear your head, and become open-minded.

What if at least 95 percent of what you have been taught all of your life is wrong?

I don't mean wrong in the sense that you will automatically think of. I use the word not in a judgmental sense but in the sense that it could all be wrong for you personally, wrong for this day and age, and wrong for this exact moment in your present circumstances.

This is something I had to face and deal with in order to begin growing into the person I wanted to be instead of the person I was told I was supposed to be.

This is an extremely hard pill to swallow for most of us, but once you really look at it from an objective point of view, you can tap into the truth. And as cliché as it may sound, it will set you free.

The thing about *wrong* is that it is such a relative term. During Prohibition, people could be sentenced to prison for doing what many of us do on a regular basis. What is legal in Amsterdam will get you thrown in jail in many other countries. What was legally justified by the Rules Of Engagement in combat, would get men put on death row in the peace time. The point is that *wrong* is a very relative and subjective term.

So what do I mean when I say that everything we have ever learned could be wrong? Very simply put, if I have not sought my own truth about a certain person, place, organization, institution, presidential candidate, country, ethnicity, period of history, who or what God is, and the like, then it is a fact that I am operating and relying on what others tell and teach me. I am seeing the world through their eyes. It is my experience that the bulk of our population lacks the wherewithal to seek individual truth. We want to be told how to feel, how to think, who to vote for, why things are bad, and who is to blame, and when we choose to behave like this, we place the burden of responsibility on "them" when, chances are, we don't know much about "them." By the way, this mind-set enables this class of person to easily and comfortably assume the victim role, which is rocket fuel for the terminal uniqueness I spoke of and suffered with.

I realized that the only way to live freely was to make sure that every ounce of my life was grounded in a belief or point of view that I had created or agreed with through my own research. Then and only then could I take responsibility for my present circumstances and, in doing so, effect positive change in my life.

Chapter Four

Thinking for Yourself

Parts of this concept were covered in the previous chapter, but its importance is so huge that I wanted to spend some more time explaining how deciding to live this way continues to improve my quality of life.

The next time you have the opportunity to spend some time with a toddler, please pay close attention to the actions they take and the manner in which they conduct their lives. You will quickly see several things:

- They need only the basic necessities of life to be content.
- They never ask permission before trying something new.
- They are in a state of shock when someone gets between them and a new desire or adventure.
- They laugh with such enthusiasm that they infect all in their presence with true joy.

As always, the list could continue, but the takeaway for me is very simple: children have minds of their own, and they think for themselves. So how, when, and where does this freedom begin to erode into rigid boundaries that are held together with the fears of our parents, teachers, or society? When do we put on the yoke of fear and chains of mediocrity?

It's simple: we put those things on when we are told to by certain people who are major influences in our lives. These people are nothing short of our "gods." Their intentions are always best—according to them and from their perspectives—but what if they are only passing on a set of chains that were placed on them many years ago by their gods, who were also doing the best they could during that time, under those conditions, and in accordance with their perspectives? What if the best that they could do for us was not enough, or not what we need right now?

We so readily assign others' perceptions or opinions to the many thoughts and decisions in our lives—especially the big ones—and we choose to think for ourselves on the "little things." This takes the burden of responsibility off of our backs and places it on the shoulders of those who seek to "help us" or manipulate us. If they turn out to be wrong, then we can blame them; if they turn out to be right, we can take credit for the success as long as they don't find out we are frauds. To many, this is a recipe for life that they believe to be the acceptable. I say it is the mire that keeps them from becoming the people they are capable of being.

Another one of fear's many faces that keeps us from thinking for ourselves is the state of being needy. When I feel I need someone or something in order to live, I am very likely to never speak my mind (think for myself) for fear of losing what I am certain that I need. This state of needing creates a vicious cycle of fear, guilt, anger, shame, and hopelessness, all for my desire to hold onto something that, I am sure, if lost would be devastating. For example: If I lost my job, my wife, or any other person place or thing, my life would suck. I can tell you that lived life this way for many years, and it is a recipe for turmoil and sickness, both mental and physical.

When I live my life believing that my world will end without any certain person place or thing, I am destined to live in a constant state of panic and fear. For me, this panic and fear led to physical sickness. I suffered for many years with Irritable Bowel Syndrome (IBS), chronic fatigue, fibromyalgia, sleep disorder and several other ailments due to this fear and panic. I had to learn to think for myself, and come to believe that although it would be great to have some of what I desired in life, I had to become willing to loose all of it, and in coming to grips with this reality I could then begin to think for myself, and in doing so, free myself from the bondage of false fears.

Desire anything you want in this world, but never be in need of it, for if you do, you will surely go without, and going without, you will live a lifetime of disappointment and resentment.

Chapter Five

Standing Tall All Alone

It is common for folks to say that they have high moral standards and that they will always make the right decisions in life. How many times have we all sworn that we would not listen to the masses and what they have to say about what we should think or how we should act?

How many times in my life have I wished that I had the courage to "do the right thing"? Thousands! How many times did I feel my gut churning as I made poor decisions based on what "they" said? Thousands!

Why is it that the old adage "Hard right over the easy wrong" was so true in my life?

Simply put, I was not comfortable standing tall all alone. Please notice that I inserted the word *tall*, not leaving just *alone*. The implications of the word *tall* are huge. This implies that we not only choose to go against the grain or do the right thing and make the hard choice but that we do this with confidence and zero regret. It is easy to do the right thing and then mope, talking about how boring it made things, how the world should reward us for our grand deeds, or how much fun everyone else is having.

It is only the hard right when I am uncomfortable in my own skin. The right thing was too hard to do only when I was more concerned with what others thought and what others said or might say. You see, I will always choose the easy wrong as long as I am more afraid of what others think than I am of the consequences of wrong or poor decisions. The need to belong to something larger than ourselves has driven many good people to do things that they never would have done if they had the courage to stand tall all alone.

This mind set was very true in my life during my younger years. I was so afraid of what people thought of me, and I rarely thought twice about decisions that caused me or another person pain, as long as I thought the outcome would make me feel like the center of attention, or part of the "cool click". My judgment was easily swayed by a comment or thought of what others may think about whom I was as a person, based off of me doing something or not doing something. I am currently not immune to thinking like this, nor will I ever be immune to this thought process; for this is the work of my ego, and my ego will always win unless kept right sized. I have to do the work of ego deflation on a daily basis if I am to have the courage to make my own path in life and stay comfortable in my own skin.

Chapter Six
Law of Attraction

Simply put, whatever I hold in my conscious and subconscious mind for a period of time will somehow and someway manifest in my life on the physical plane. This applies to both the good and the bad, according to one's perception.

I have no intention, nor do I possess ample knowledge, to cover the intricate details of such a complex topic. Numerous books have already been written about the law of attraction, many of which I have read and suggest that you read if interested.

This is a lesson—or as I have come to agree, a law—that is always at work in my life. The excessive publicity on this law as it relates to financial wealth has turned many people away from finding their own truth about it and thereby closed their minds to the theory. This is very unfortunate because there is so much more to be gained for the knowledge gained about this power.

The most important aspect of the law of attraction (in my opinion) is that it is always at work—that means twenty-four/ seven—which has huge implications. That means that I am manifesting my reality with every single thought that enters my mind. Should you ever choose to believe that this law is real, as I have, you will then understand what it means to take full and absolute responsibility for the circumstances of your current life situation. That is what that knowledge did and does for me. It reminds me that I am responsible for what is going on in my life, good, bad, or otherwise.

In closing, this theory or law is one that I have come to believe with all of my heart. There is much written about the mind's ability to manifest matter. I encourage you to find out your own truth about this concept. You have nothing to lose and much to gain should you take the time to learn of this universal power.

Chapter Seven

Figuring Out the Source

The source of what? You might ask. I am referring to the source of each and every thing that is in your life, be it good, bad, temporary, pleasant, painful, and so on.

This statement can be viewed as both very simple and very complex. For me, it bounces back and forth between the two.

From the time I joined the US Army at seventeen years old until the day I chose to seek out the answer to this very question, the source of almost everything in my life was the US Army. Whatever didn't fit into those categories, I placed on the rest of those who were close to me—my wife, friends, coworkers, and myself. I associated who I was as a person with what I did for a living by saying I was a soldier, a paratrooper, a Green Beret. But none of those were really who I was. They were just more false truths, more commonly known as lies. The problem with this lie was that I was living it and had convinced myself that it was true. As I mentioned before, my source was not just the army; the source of my happiness was often alcohol, my wife, my friends, and myself. I lived this way for many years with a moderate to high level of "perceived" happiness, but all of these sources have one thing in common: they all can, and will, dry up. And when they did, I was left hopeless, for what else was there to place my hope in once all of my sources failed me and I had miserably failed myself?

If my wife, job, boss, or friend is the source of my happiness, then how I feel each day is contingent upon their day went. This arrangement is, first, a very sick way to live and, second, a cowardly way to live.

The sick part is more obvious than the cowardly part, so I'll explain: If I make a conscious decision to place my happiness, financial security, or the like in the hands of anyone but myself, I will always be able to play the role of the victim by placing the blame on that which I have designated as my source. This keeps me in a vicious cycle of blaming, living in the past, and justifying my anger while never taking responsibility for my present circumstances. This is a recipe for cowardice, long-term misery, and a stagnant spirit.

So what is the source?

I don't know what the answer is for you, but I can say with confidence that if it is a friend, hobby, job, spouse, drug, institution, or the like, you are set up for many disappointments. Although this may come off as being a bit presumptuous about your future, I can make that statement with confidence because I have lived it, and I have felt the gut wrenching emotion of regret and resentment when that which I "made" my source, continued to fail me.

Each of us has our own journey, and on it, we decide to either seek our own truth to this question or not. I can tell you that for me, the search required many years of hard questions, long conversations, and countless hours of reading and research. This is not to say that you will need to spend all of the time and effort that I did; this is just how it was for me.

In my life, there are actually two sources—one is the source of all my trouble, and the other is the source of all that is good. The first source is me, making decisions based on self and suffering consequences that I view as bad. The second source is a higher power that I call God. Life is pretty simple when viewed through this lens, and it makes for simple answers to complex questions and situations.

I had to find a source that would never dry up, fail me, or let me down. That is the only way that I can ensure that I will always have more of what it is that I need. Once I was able to believe to my core that God was the source of everything good in my life and that my poor, selfish decisions were the source of all that was bad in my life, I no longer had to be concerned with anything or anyone else. There is a wise question that I stole from my brother many years ago that I would like to share with you: When in any situation that could be viewed as bad or unfortunate, he would ask himself, "Have I lied, cheated, stolen, or manipulated anything to create the circumstances in question?" If the answer was no, then it was all meant to be. If the answer was yes, then he made it that way. Both answers provide that oh-so-important information that I spoke of early on: the "why." If I have lied, cheated, stolen, or manipulated anything, then that is why I am in a shitty situation. On the other hand, if I have done all that is right and things are still looking grim, the answer to the why is that it is meant to be this way. Either way, I get clarity and can accurately assign responsibility.

I'll close this chapter by circling back to the last few chapters. I had to become willing to think for myself, ask the hard questions, undo years of wrong thinking, and prepared to stand alone on my journey to finding my source, and in finding my source I was granted the true freedom that is meant to be had by all.

Chapter Eight

There *Is* Enough for Everyone

There is enough of everything for everyone. This may seem like an overly simplistic feel-good statement, and that's is because it is. No gimmicks; no gotchas. Once I figured this out, there was no longer a lack of anything in my life. Once I figured out my source, this became clear immediately. You can believe it or not. I chose and continue to choose to believe that it is true, and the results of this mind-set are clearly displayed in my life. They can be in yours, too, if you so choose.

The constant mantra of "there is not enough" is one that is very popular in this day and age. This statement of lack is one that creates jealousy, resentment, and feelings of being victimized by those who have more. Just as I said at the beginning of the book, we are all different in many aspects, and this is one of those aspects. We all have a different picture of what happiness looks or feels like. What the word *happy* means to me may be something entirely different than it means to you. Not everyone wants the pie-in-the-sky mansion or the celebrity status. We all have our own individual hopes and dreams. In my opinion, it is not a matter of not having enough for everyone; it is a matter of everyone not having enough courage and faith to go after what it is they desire. There is a recurring trend here, and it leads back to fear. Everything starts from one of two places—fear or love—and the "there is not enough" idea is deeply rooted in fear.

For me, this ties right back into the law of attraction. If my thoughts are that there is not enough, then that will be the case, for what I hold in mind long enough will manifest itself into the matter of my life. A great analogy was shared with me about belief in something that is unseen or incomprehensible, both being terms to describe the law of attraction: "If you meet an Aboriginal elder from the outback who has never seen a light other than the sun or the moon, has never been out of the bush, and has no concept of electricity, and you take her to a room with a light switch in it, close the door to create total darkness, and tell her that when she flips the switch, she will make the room as bright as sunshine, she will stare at you in disbelief and swear that it is impossible. But when she flips the switch, the light comes on anyway." The moral to the story is that neither the light bulb nor the electrical current running through the wires care about what this elder thinks or believes, for when she flips the switch, the light will come on in spite of her disbelief. This, I propose to you, is how the law of attraction works. It couldn't care less about what I believe because, in spite of what I think, it is working in perfect synchronicity with the thoughts in my head. I hope I have caused you to think hard about this theory, and I hope you seek your own truth of its power.

Chapter Nine

The True Meaning of Courage

My experience-based opinion on this subject is something that I believe is worth sharing with you because, more often than not, I see this word misused, misunderstood, and poorly represented.

Let's first talk about what courage isn't in order to highlight what it is. Courage is not:

- The total and complete absence of fear
- Screaming like a madman or madwoman in the face of fear
- Betting your life savings on a long-shot deal
- Possessing the proverbial "balls the size of church bells"

So if courage is none of the above, what is it? In my opinion, it is the total and complete ability to outmatch fear with overwhelming faith in a power greater than that of any human and for me that means God.

There is an extreme difference between living in fear and walking dignified and comfortably through it.

So how, you may ask, does one walk comfortably and peacefully through the most horrific tragedies that life has to offer? I'll do my best to answer that question as it relates to my life and, in doing so, hopefully provide a frame of reference for you to find the same or greater courage than I have, should you choose to take the required actions.

When is the last time you asked yourself, "What am I afraid of?" If it has been a while, you may want to do so immediately. Answering this requires you to get honest, and if you are incapable of being honest with yourself, then you are incapable of learning what true courage is.

I ask myself this question very often, and in the times that I forget to ask; I am lucky enough to have many people close to me who will ask me. Whether the question comes from me or another, the effect remains the same: to answer it, I have to pinpoint what it is that I am afraid of before I can tap into the required courage to face it.

I have been taught that there are only two emotions in the human experience: love and fear. You may be thinking, *That's a lie. We have literally hundreds of words to describe our emotions and feelings.* But all of those words are merely grander expressions of either love or fear.

This is a good time to interject a topic that will be talked about in greater detail later in the book, and it is one that entire books have been written about—the theory of all things being relative only to that which they are not.

The theory that there are only two "core" emotions in the human experience is made clear only when you understand that you must first know what you are not before you will know what you are. This concept holds true for every single thing in our lives. Hot is made relative only by the cold, light is made relative only by the dark, and love is made relevant only by fear.

26

Love is the more obvious core emotion of the two and requires little explanation; therefore, I will spend no more time explaining how joy, happiness, sweetness, elation, and so on can be tied back to their root or core, which is love.

Now for examining the fear factor. Fear has many faces, some of the more common ones being hate, rage, anger, resentment, panic, paranoia, stress, and anxiety. Most folks (myself included) would much rather say, "I am so pissed at Jim for interrupting me at the board meeting yesterday" than say, "I am so afraid that the CEO is going to think I am a weak leader because Jim talked about his idea out of turn, and I am responsible for Jim's behavior." The first statement allows the person I am talking to to justify my anger and get on my side. The second answer forces me to admit that I am scared that I may not get the end-of-year bonus because of what the boss may now think of me.

Fear has driven me to do things that I thought were well beneath me and to speak of and to others in a fashion that I soon regretted. Those who have not the courage provided by faith often do drastic things that are driven by their fear. I'll say that again—*drastic* things driven by *fear*. Every bad decision, every regret—I mean, every single thing in my life that can be viewed as having been a bad call on my part—was driven by some form of fear. I had to come to grips with this truth and take the actions required to begin to have a newfound courage that would keep these dramatic episodes from continuing to occur.

What is fear stealing from you?

Chapter Ten

Take Care of You First

The title of this chapter has created and will always create controversy, so let's take care of that right away. This statement must be properly framed and seen from the proper perspective to be understood in the context that I mean it. This is not a free pass to shrink from the responsibilities that you have chosen to take on—your children, your spouse, your job, and so on. This does not mean that I will allow others to suffer while I take care of my wants and desires, being selfish, self-serving, and cruel, which is not what I am speaking of or something I would ever advocate.

Simply put, I cannot give away what I do not possess. Just like many of you reading this book, I was often taught that I needed to give, give, give to help others, to sacrifice for others, and that it would all come back to me in the end. I have come to believe that this is all very misguided advice and circles back to an earlier chapter about figuring out that much of what I have been taught was wrong.

On the surface, the theory of putting others first, sacrificing for others and always giving, sounds very "saintly," which many would love to be branded. The problem/fact is that there are many who live according to these principles and never achieve sainthood. In fact, they end up at the opposite end of the spectrum—anger-filled, resentment-infested, neurotic, codependent, drama-ridden, narcissistic, depressed, and broken human beings, which I believe happens because their acts of kindness come from a mindset of "sacrifice" and not love.

The key factor in the decisions we make to help, give, or share is motive, which is grounded in one of the two emotions that exist: fear or love. When we give from the root of fear (a.k.a. obligation or sacrifice), the outcome and meaning of the gift are lost long before it is even given. Fear-driven sacrifices or gifts merely set the stage for future disappointment, remorse, regret, resentment, and drama, which is what the fearful "giver" subconsciously desires. Does this setup sound sick? You bet it does, because in this scenario, that is exactly the case: only a sick human would live such a life. This describes a life full of broken expectations and nothing more. There is a cure for this sickness, and it is nothing less than pure love. It starts with the love of oneself. When we put the task of keeping ourselves "full" in the hands of other humans, we are doomed to live a miserable life because—guess what— they are more concerned with their needs than yours. And, yes, this applies to your family members and closest friend.

The decision to take care of yourself first is never selfish when the motive for doing so is grounded in love. I have come to realize that my needs (not wants) have to be taken care of before I am able to give anything that is worth receiving. If I am filled up, I no longer look for what I can take from the world. I no longer feel hollow inside, and I no longer need anything. So what are the needs that take such a priority over the needs of those I love and who depend on me? I'll give you my list, which may or may not line up with yours. So don't compare; just try to relate.

The ultimate need that I have is to feel secure in every aspect of life. The only way I can guarantee that this need is taken care of on a daily basis is to take that responsibility out of the hands of those who cannot provide it and place it in the hands of something that must be greater than any human. It is only then that my expectations and needs will be met. It is not my place to tell you what this power is for you, so I will not be so arrogant as to lecture you on God, spirituality, religion, or the like. I am merely stating a fact: if I give this responsibility of maintaining my happiness and security to any human or many humans, I will be very disappointed—and this is not opinion; it is fact.

I have lived a life of placing expectations on others to make me feel secure, and I have suffered the consequences of this path. As a result, I have chosen to never again walk this path. The God that I have come to know and love takes care of this need now and always will. It's that simple. I have started with this need first for a reason, for from love of self, stems all that is good. So what do you have to do to get to a place of being totally secure? It has nothing to do with getting more of and everything to do with getting rid of.

I had to get rid of many things in my life in order to clear a path that led to me having the ability to love myself. My life was full of things that blocked me from this need. I'll give you a quick description of the steps I had to take in order to achieve the security I craved.

First, I had to be "selfish" enough to take the required time and make the effort to uncover the things that were blocking my path of self love. Once I was able to uncover these things, I then had to make the decision to be "selfish" enough to take the time to deal with them, after which I had to be "selfish" enough to "take" the time and expend the energy required to rid myself of these things. Finally, I had to be "selfish" enough to "take" the time and make the effort to continue to grow as a person, now on a different path, in a new and different life.

Please pay special attention to how many times I used the words *selfish* and *take*. This is because the process of getting rid of the obstacles in my life required me to be selfish and take, not be selfless and give.

What I have "taken" from those I love in order to complete this process is time. Taking this time is valid and necessary. I must be selfish enough to take the time required to start and finish the necessary actions that will allow me to stay rid of the things that stand between me and the source of my security and happiness. Once the process is complete and I am secure in every sense of the word, then and only then can I give back in the true spirit of the word *give, and have zero expectations after giving.*

I have successfully used this process in finding freedom from addiction, feelings of loneliness, feelings of being unfulfilled, feeling lost, feeling confused, feeling angry, feeling like I was supposed to doing something else, feeling like I was supposed to be somewhere else, feeling like I was in the wrong career, feeling like the world was against me, feeling like it was all "their" fault, and feeling like a victim who couldn't catch a break. I had to be selfish enough to take the time to do the work required, which has in turn enabled me to live a life filled with security and happiness that is dependent on no one but me and my God. This love of self first is the key to freedom and the ability to give to others with no thought of obligation, fear, or sacrifice. You see, the minute that I feel I am sacrificing for you is the minute that I move out of love and into fear, for love doesn't know sacrifice and expects nothing in return. This is only because I cannot *need* when I am filled with love to begin with.

An entire book can be, and has been, written on this subject, so I will belabor the point no longer. Love yourself enough to take until you are fit to give.

Chapter Eleven

Expectations

I want to share with you this short definition of the word *expectations*, according to me: A predestined time in the not-so-distant future when you will be absolutely and utterly disappointed by the person, place, or institution that the expectation or expectations have been placed upon. Count on it!

The majority of the frustrations I have in life start with this single word. The minute that I place expectations on anything, I am screwed. There is only one me; therefore, there is only one person who thinks and acts like me, only one person who has my morals and rules, and that person is me.

If I could burn something into my brain, it would be the last two paragraphs. If I could recall this wisdom before every human encounter I have, my life would be so much more enjoyable, but I can't, so I still struggle.

The takeaway from this lesson is very simple. People will almost never act, say, do, think, give, take, or do anything else the way I would expect them to. Since "almost never" is accurate, I would be best served to assume that "never" would be the case and let myself be pleasantly surprised with any positive outcomes.

Now to confuse you for a moment. I just got done telling you that if I expect anything from any person place or thing, that I was setting the stage for a huge disappointment, right? And I believe that to be true. I also believe that when I am living a life that is grounded in a faith of my choosing, with a God of my choosing as my source for all that I am, and all that have, I can have huge expectations about how great my life is, and always will be, and never be let down. What may sound like a contradiction is what I have come to know as a truth, for expectations of abundance, prosperity, health and happiness are safe and believable when placed in the hands of a God that I have unwavering faith in. I have come to learn and believe that are many concepts in this life that appear to be contradictions, but I have found they are just two truths, that work in perfect harmony, in their own unique way.

Chapter Twelve

The Surrender

The word *surrender* immediately plants an image of *beaten, losing, lost, weak, subservient, less than, small*, or a host of any other adjectives that would paint a picture in your head of the exact opposite of what it is I will be talking about next.

Granted, this is not new material, nor a topic that has not been addressed by many over the years, but the impact of this action (not word) is so profound that I have to give you my take on it, so here goes.

For starters, I am not referring to surrender in the obvious sense of the word. All of the following information should not be looked at from a literal perspective but from more of a symbolic perspective. This surrender I speak of happens in the mind of a tortured soul, not on a literal field of battle.

I was taught, like so many others, to never surrender, never quit. Again, this falls into the category of all of that great stuff I was taught that was either not true or not applicable to my present circumstances.

Before I can effectively talk about the action of surrender and where it can be the best strategy for victory, I have to talk about the path that leads to the circumstances that provide the opportunity for surrender.

The first item on that path is an admission that I am powerless. Over what? You may ask. Everything! Well, not quite everything, because I do have power over my thoughts, which dictate my actions, but that is as far as the power goes. Once I truly embrace this reality and am placed in a state of willingness, which is made possible only by my admitted inability to control the world, then and only then am I ready for the action of surrendering.

I surrender only when I have exhausted all means possible to achieve victory and am still losing. Even then, I have an option other than surrender, which so many have chosen—death. Fortunately for me, I did not go that route, and it is my hope that this book may help many people see that death is not necessary to ease the pain and that they too can achieve happiness and success by surrendering.

The action of surrendering places us in an unbelievably vulnerable state. A state that is foreign to us, and that goes against every single cell of our genetic code, and, moreover, places our egos in the worst-case scenario, which is where the real problem lies. You see, the ego does not care about the pain and turmoil; it only cares about what others may think, how we will look, or a litany of other bullshit reasons that the ego so readily shouts to our soul.

So what this means is that I have to become totally beat down to the point that not even my arrogance has a dog in the fight, and let me tell you, for a guy like me, that is saying something.

My first experience with the absolute and total success of surrendering was when I was honestly facing my alcoholism. I was told that in order to achieve victory over the illness of alcoholism (from which I definitely suffered), I had to surrender, and that before I could truly surrender, I had to make an admission to my core that I was powerless over alcohol and put myself in a constant and total state of willingness to do anything required. Then I had to surrender my life to something greater than me. As it was simply put, "Scot, all you need to know is that there is a God, and you ain't it." This is not a book on how to get sober, nor will I continue discussing my journey through recovery. This is nothing more than my first success in surrender and one that I came to repeat many times between then and now.

You see, this process of becoming beaten down, admitting I had no power, becoming willing to try anything, and surrendering my stubborn will can and should be applied to every aspect of my life—that's right, 100 percent of the time—because the fastest and easiest way for me to win is to surrender. Now I want to make clear that this act of surrender does not come without a hell of a workload, which is why I have emphasized the "action" of surrender, for the word *surrender* without action provides nothing of substance or consequence.

So you may say, "If there are so many instances when this surrender will work, why doesn't everyone live this way?" The answer is one simple word—ego. These three little letters stand in the way of surrender. This is what requires the beatings to be so severe, the depression to be so great, and the suffering to last so long. The bitch of it is that we are rarely taught this truth. In fact, for most of us, absolutely the only way we can obtain this knowledge is to quite literally die inside, for it is then that we become willing to live again.

For the record, I am not great at this whole surrender thing. I struggle daily with it, but my pain threshold gets much lower with each struggle in my life, and that is progress that I can live with. I used to run full steam, headfirst into the same brick wall twenty to thirty times; now I usually stop at ten or so!

Although this action of surrendering can be applied to every aspect of my life, I know it is not necessary to bore you with those details, but I do want to highlight its importance when it comes to my spirituality, which is where the act of surrendering is necessary on a daily basis if I am to live happy, joyous, and free.

It is impossible for me, or anyone for that matter, to live a faith-based life without a daily act of surrender. Several years ago, I heard the best analogy to describe a faith-based life: An old, wise man sat down beside a young lad in the front row, under the shade of the Big Top Circus tent. They made small talk as they anxiously awaited the next tightrope extravaganza. High above the crowd, the performer stood on the platform. In front of the performer stood an empty wheelbarrow that he obviously intended to push across the tightrope. There was no net, and the tension in the tent was palpable, matched only by a silence that was deafening. In the moments before the performer advanced onto the rope, the old, wise man nudged the young lad and asked, "Do you think he's going to make it across?" to which the young man replied confidently, "Of course, he will." "How can you be so sure?" replied the old, wise man. "Because he has done this at least a thousand times, and it is what he must do on a daily basis," replied the young lad. The old, wise man smiled and asked, "Are you certain of this?" and the young lad replied, "110 percent sure." With that, the old, wise man replied, "So how about you go get in the wheelbarrow?"

This story sums up life for me. I am either out of the wheelbarrow and in control, or I am in the wheelbarrow and out of control. It is easy to *say* that I am going to trust in my God, yet it is a completely different thing to put actions with my words and get in the wheelbarrow. To become helpless and vulnerable, to trust without reservation, to take the actual (not hypothetical) "leap of faith" is something very few can follow through with. I have taken many leaps of faith in my life, and I can tell you that there is no sweeter feeling than to be pushed across the tightrope to the new platform of safety, having nothing to do with the success other than getting in the wheelbarrow. Effortless success—now that is something worth looking into.

I want you to know that every day is a new moment in time, and I have to wake up and make a decision whether to live that moment and those to follow as either the stressed-out, scared performer pushing the wheelbarrow or the calm and relaxed passenger moving forward without effort. The degree of my ability to become the passenger is in direct proportion to my ability to completely and totally surrender to my God. Many people like to speak of and philosophize about taking a personal leap of faith or living by faith, but very few take the action necessary to reap the wealth and happiness that such an act will provide.

So it is a simple question: Have you surrendered, or are you still the shaky-kneed, stressed-out, scared performer, focused on nothing but the hard ground below?

Chapter Thirteen

Healthy Walls and Boundaries

I was often taught that I should not build walls of isolation, that I should stay open to others' opinions, and that what others wanted to bring into my life should be welcomed, and I do not want to be rude to those who were just trying to help or guide me through life and the decisions made during it. It is my experience, though, that living this way makes for one hell of a confusing life—in fact, one that is destined to be filled with a great many disappointments.

The ability to erect healthy walls and boundaries requires almost all of what I have talked about in the previous chapters. I have to be comfortable and at peace all by myself, I have to have the courage to think on my own, I have to be willing to shoulder the responsibility that comes with these decisions, I have to take care of me first, and I have to understand and be willing to accept the consequences of taking these actions; for it is only then that I will be able to rest easy, knowing that I have kept certain people, even those who claim to love and care for me, out of my life.

This is an extremely hard pill to swallow. It goes against all that

I have been taught. This gets back into the whole sacrifice crap that I was taught, but as I said before, love knows no sacrifice, so if there is sacrifice involved, love is not the driving force.

I could talk about many areas of my life where it makes sense to have the boundaries that I speak of, but I'll focus on the four that are most important for me, which are my faith, my family, my friends, and my career.

My faith is the first on the list because I know that, without it, I would not have my family, friends, or a career. So what kind of walls or boundaries do I set up to help maintain my faith? Well, before I could set up these boundaries, I had to have none of them. I had to be open and willing to allow all people to share their wisdom and thoughts with me. I had to be open and honest in conversations with those who wanted me to join their "camp." I had to explore every nook and cranny, read every book, listen to every lecture, and digest all of the information I gathered, and it was then that I could choose my brand of faith and set up the walls and boundaries necessary for me to maintain and grow in this faith. This meant that I had to be done asking the hard questions, reading all of the books that were outside of what I chose to believe, and listening to those who believed something outside of what I had chosen to believe. This did not mean that I chose to disassociate with all who didn't think or believe like me; I just chose not to bring up this topic in our conversation and asked that they do the same unless they were interested in what I believed. You see, I had to take myself "off the market," so to speak, for I was no longer shopping or buying anything, and I had nothing to sell. It is important for me to keep those who would make fun of or ridicule my faith out of my life and allow in only those who support and accept my faith, whether they agree with it or not. This may seem drastic, but for me it is necessary.

Now to my family, which seems to be the hardest and most

painful place to execute these necessary actions. The process of setting up healthy walls and boundaries is the same here. I had to be open to all, and for many years, before I could discern for myself whose advice was relevant, whose love was unconditional, and whose opinion mattered. Once I took the actions necessary to think for myself, took responsibility for my own well-being, and became willing to accept full responsibility for the consequences of these healthy walls and boundaries, I could choose to exclude the others.

In the beginning, there was only me to take care of, which was pretty simple, but when I chose to get married and have kids, this situation became a bit complex! I had to choose to take responsibility for the well-being of my family, which I define as my wife and two children.

The rules are very simple when it comes to my family: If someone or something brings any drama, suffering, or discomfort of any kind into our family unit, I place that someone or something outside the barrier or wall. If, on the other end of the spectrum, someone chooses to bring additional love and support to our family unit, that person stays inside the wall or boundary. These rules come with consequences, so I think it is important to talk about them.

First, the positive aspects: my spouse knows that our family's happiness and security are the most important things to me, and my children live a life surrounded by those who love and care for them. My family stays out of the drama of others, and we all live a happier and more content life. Now for the other consequences—and notice that I did not call them bad or negative, just "other." Family members who fall on the outside of these boundaries may have their feelings hurt, they may attempt to take out their frustrations on members of my family, they may gossip about the choices I have made, and they may choose to never again speak to me or members of my family. These are all decisions that are out of my control and nothing more than their choices, in which I have no say. Remember my rules, and you will see why the decisions that they make are of no concern to me. Once I choose to take responsibility for taking care of the well-being of my family unit, these decisions are easy. The only time they become difficult is when I take responsibility for the happiness of those outside of my immediate family unit, which makes for a prime-time setup of manipulation and discord at the expense of my family. I have to remember that it is not my responsibility to keep my dad, mom, sister, brother, brother-in-law, sister-in-law, grandmother, or the like happy. As I pointed out before, if they place expectations on me that will set the stage for them being unhappy or happy, they are the ones who will be disappointed, and it is their choice and fault. They have their own family units to take care of, and what we do in ours is none of their business until we choose to make it their business. This way of living is not cold, nor is it rude. It is taking care of those you are responsible for and nothing less than love.

The rules set forth for family members are also applied to my friends and associates, so there's no need to go over them again here.

You may find it odd that I listed my profession in this list of areas that require healthy walls and boundaries, but I believe it is extremely important. Here are the facts as I have experienced them.

Most people are unhappy in the careers that they have currently. Most people do not have the courage required to make life-changing decisions that would bring them to careers they would love. Most people have chosen a career because it is what others have expected of them. Most people stay in a career that they hate for the sake of the perceived safety that it provides. Most people live on self-will and are unwilling to get into the wheelbarrow. Most people have a very strong opinion of what you and I should do with our lives.

Most people believe they know what is best for us. Well, let me be the first to tell you that I am not most people, and neither are you.

If I had chosen to continue to listen to what others thought I should do, I would not be as happy and free as I am today, and I definitely would not be writing this book. You see, misery loves company, and their egos create in them a need to be heard and to be right. In making choices that I have made for my career, I have had family members stop speaking to me, friends who have called me stupid, coworkers who have called me a quitter, and on and on and on, but what they think does not matter to me. Now let me tell you—there were many years that I listened to what they thought, and just like I laid out in the path to surrender, I had to become sick and tired of living the life they chose for me before I could choose for myself. Then I had to get into the wheelbarrow and take actions that were only as strong as my faith. You see the trend here: choosing to make these boundaries requires that I listen to all, gather the information, sift out the good, block or remove the bad, and move forward. Once I determine who is a supporter and who is not, once I have been shown who is in my corner no matter what, then it becomes obvious whom I should be listening to, if anyone. The consequences of putting up these walls and boundaries are earth shattering and life changing. I remove from my life the "negative Nellies" and surround myself with those who are more concerned with my happiness than with their opinions on my decisions. I have to stack the deck in my favor; if I don't, I will lose, and to me, being in a career that I am not passionate about is nothing short of losing.

In summary, many walls and boundaries are necessary to help maintain my family's well-being and my personal well-being. The road to placing these boundaries requires thought, discernment, courage, and the ability to accept the "other" consequences of placing them. It is very simple: neither my family nor I will be held hostage by the actions, manipulations, selfish acts, or opinions of those who do not have our or my happiness as the driving force behind their actions. Always overlook what others are saying but never lose sight of what they are doing, for it is in their actions that they tell you their truth.

Chapter Fourteen

The Power of Your Environment

An old adage says that if you sit in a barbershop long enough, you'll end up with a haircut. You can change the word *barbershop* to the local bar, a nightclub, or a used car lot, for that matter, and sooner rather than later, you will indeed drink too much, get in a fight, get a DUI, lead a promiscuous sex life, or buy a car. It's just the way it goes. The human psyche and the desire to fit in will overrule common sense at some point.

It shouldn't be a surprise when any of these events happen because each place I mentioned is there specifically to facilitate these end states. The fault lies not with the bar owner or the pretty guy, gal, or used car salesman; it lies with us for ever frequenting these establishments in the first place. I know I am being a bit over the top with these analogies, but it is to make a valid point about the places where we choose to spend our time. Now to the people.

The choice of people who we surround ourselves with is of the utmost importance and requires constant evaluation of where we are on our journey and, more important, where we want to be. Separating ourselves from the people in our lives who were or are negative requires a level of determination and brutal honesty that is made possible only by a strong faith, belief system, love of self, and desire to be at peace. You see, if my desire to be at total peace and ease is less powerful than my desire to be liked, loved, or part of the in crowd, then I will always put up with people in my life who cause the discontent I feel in my soul. This comes back to the most simplistic of laws: cause and effect.

If I have someone in my life that causes me to feel drained, guilty, or anything less than at peace, I have the choice to remove myself from the unhealthy relationship. I can do this only if I love myself more than I love the other person's feelings. Isn't that what it is always about?

In my opinion, there is no such thing as "brutal honesty," only honesty. The part that is considered brutal is the emotion that a person has in response to an honest or factual statement. How an individual reacts to what I may state as fact or opinion is not of my concern; as I have said, I can control only my own thoughts, so what another thinks is up to them and none of my business. In fact, the other individual has the right to remove me from their life until they think I can have a positive effect on them. It's their choice, not mine, and it's simple cause and effect in perfect harmony.

Now, many people would jump to conclusions at this point and say that I am writing everyone in the world a blank check to be a jerk in the name of honesty, and yes, I am, but the same laws of cause and effect apply to the jerks of the world. When they choose to be honest in a circumstance when the honesty will surely cause them to be hated, then the jerk who is being honest will reap the consequences of his actions. Am I saying that it is better to lie to someone if you think that being honest will cause damage? No, that is not what I am saying at all.

What I am saying is that honesty is just that and nothing more, and it is in direct correlation to an individual's perspective and relative to each of the parties involved, which makes for extremely complex situations. It will be up to you to figure out these situations. I do know this: when my honesty comes from a place of love and caring, it can never do harm. It may cause some tension or an uncomfortable spell, but good always comes of it. Now, when my honesty comes from a place of "being right" or frustration, it will almost always lead to a long, drawn-out sequence of conversations in which I have to do my best to justify my honesty—or as my wife calls it, being a jerk.

So it may look like I have gotten off topic here, and maybe I have, but the gist of it all is that I will have many opportunities in my life to decide if being honest enough with someone to remove them from my life is worth the effect produced by the honesty. And it will be only through love of self and others (in that order) that I will make the right decision. All of life is made up of choices followed by actions, which are followed by reactions. I am responsible only for my choice, my action, and my response to the reaction.

For example, If Aunt Sophie, Uncle Manny, your husband's dad, your mom, or any other person is coming over for an occasion at your house and you and everyone else knows that when this person gets there, things will be different—drama may occur, the night will become all about them, your kids will have a bad example around, and the like—it will only be through faith, love of self, and love of others that you will have the courage to do what is best for all parties involved. Otherwise, you will cower behind the cloak of fear and anxiety, claiming that this person's feelings are more important than your family's or your happiness. Sickening and sad, isn't it? Yet it happens all the time.

I like to call these special people "hostage takers." Just like all the criminals in the world, they are absolutely justified in the crimes that they commit. They believe that they have every right to feel the way that they feel and to take the actions that they take.

These people will hold their victims hostage for a lifetime if allowed, and that word—*allowed*—is the key to the whole situation. When we allow the known hostage taker to consistently ruin Christmas dinners, our kids' birthday parties, and other social events, why are we so surprised when it happens? This reminds me of a great analogy.

A little girl walking through the woods stumbles upon a very sick snake, so she picks it up to take home in order to help it get better. After two long days of making sure the snake has warmth, food, and water, the young girl leans down to give the snake a goodnight kiss , and the snake bites her right in the face. The little girl exclaimed, "After all I have done for you, how could you bite me?" The snake replied, "You knew I was a snake when you first picked me up, didn't you?"

Chapter Fifteen

You Need Other People

I should probably change the chapter title to "You Need the *Right Kind of **Other*** People." The "rightness" of these people is relevant only to you, so you must establish these parameters in accordance with where you are and where you want to go.

In order to surround myself with the right people, I must first fully understand where I am in my life and where I want to be. There is no right or wrong answer here, only my current truth based on my current thoughts and perceptions, and the same applies to you.

For me, answering the questions of where I am in life and where I want to go is a simple process. I ask myself a series of questions that are followed by decisions and actions. If I answer the questions honestly and have the courage to face the truth, I will make the right choices, the actions will produce what it is I desire, and the right people will remain in my life or begin to show up in my life.

The saying that there is strength in numbers is very true but missing one key point. I think it should be changed to, "There is strength in numbers as long as all parties are united around a common goal or mind-set." Below is a list of simple questions that I can ask myself to help me see the truth of where I am, where I want to go, and who I need around me to help in this process.

The Keepers

- Who in my life places my happiness ahead of theirs?
- Who in my life gives without expecting a return on investment?
- Who in my life wants me to succeed more than they want to be right?
- Who in my life asks me what I think is best for me?
- Who in my life is willing to share their success with me?
- Who in my life is willing to let me go my own way?
- Who in my life makes no "rules" for our relationship?
- Who in my life loves me in spite of my flaws?
- Who in my life supports my decisions?
- Who in my life is a great husband, wife, or father or mother figure?
- Who in my life is an active mentor for my personal or professional goals?
- Who in my life is depending on me for their basic needs to live?
- Who in my life looks up to me for positive reasons?
- Who in my life could benefit from my time or mentoring?

The Ones to Remove or Ignore

- Who in my life expects me to conform to their vision of life?
- Who in my life sucks the life out of me every time I am with them?

- Who in my life is always telling me I am a dreamer and that I need to be more practical?
- Who in my life is constantly in a state of drama or gossip?
- Who in my life is dependent on me for their own happiness?

These lists could have had many more questions on them, but I feel certain that you can see how easy it is to end up with very few of the right people in your life. When it comes to my relationships, I will take quality over quantity anytime. In fact, anything less puts me in a position of feeling less than fulfilled.

I have also found that the right person in one area of my life isn't necessarily the right person in every area of my life. In fact, I often screw things up when I attempt to make someone fit where he has no place, so what I really end up with are clusters of people who play a huge part in my life in the respective areas they fit into, which looks kind of like this:

- People who I can go to for spiritual guidance and or conversation
- People who I can go to for professional guidance or conversation
- People in whom I can confide the most secretive of my personal affairs
- People who I can talk to about my relationship troubles

If you are fortunate enough to have one or more people who can fill multiple roles, you are blessed. In my experience, if you find a person who fills only one role, then the responsible and smart thing to do is not to expect that person to fit into another category. Doing so will surely result in disappointment at best, or disaster at worst.

In summary, the company that we keep says volumes about who we are and where we are going. Only you can make an accurate decision on who stays and who needs to go. I wish all of you the best of luck and insurmountable clarity and courage in facing your current reality as it pertains to those whom you are allowing to influence your life.

Chapter Sixteen

Streamline with the 80/20 Principle

A principle that was first described by Italian economist Vilfredo Pareto was used to describe the disproportionate distribution of wealth in a society. Since he first uncovered such a "rule," many scholars have come to the conclusion that this ratio or close versions of this rule can be applied to almost every aspect of life. I have come to the same conclusion on my own. It is not always exactly 80/20; in fact, in some cases it may be 95/5, but it will always be close.

If this rule holds true in all of my life, then 80 percent of my problems with friends and family is coming only from 20 percent of the group. If I am in sales, this means that approximately 80 percent of my sales are coming from 20 percent of my customers, and 80 percent of my problems in the store are coming from 20 percent of the employees.

I do my best to keep this rule in mind at all times. If and when I apply it, I am able to quickly zero in on what's causing the problems or what is causing the victories. This rule is similar to the law of attraction in that it doesn't really care what we believe; it holds true in spite of our beliefs. So go ahead—take a few minutes and analyze your problems to see if you can find the 20 percent. Analyze your sales or employees to see if you can find the 20 percent in each category. Pretty amazing, isn't it? Now all you have to do is have the courage to get rid of the 20 percent that are dragging you down. That's right—get rid of them. Do it. Now!

Chapter Seventeen

FEAR

I shared with you earlier in the book that I have been taught and agree that there are only two emotions in the human psyche: fear and love. What I want to talk about here is the effect that fear has on our lives, and mine in particular.

At some point in my life, at a very young age, I allowed fear to become the driving force in my life. This is not something that I realized at the moment that it happened, and it took me many years of pain and frustration to discover and admit that I lived my life driven by fear. This does not mean that the folks who live their lives driven by love do not experience fear; it just means that their lives are not driven by it.

A wise person once said that fear ought to be classified as stealing, for fear alone will steal from you all things in life that you were supposed to have. I have come to regard that statement as one of the grandest truths that I have ever heard.

It is important to dissect something here before we go any further. I have used the word *driven* to describe how we move through life and the words *fear* and *love* to describe how we can live our lives. Let's look closer at these words to help paint this picture.

Driven—determined, single-minded, obsessed, or motivated

Fear—terror, worry, dread, horror, fright, panic, alarm

Love—feel affection for, like, adore, worship, be devoted to, care for

So here are the two choices I have when it comes to how I live my life:

1. If I live my life driven by fear, I am determined, single-minded and obsessed with the terror of what might happen, the worry of all that could happen, the dread of what I know will happen, the horror of everything going wrong, the fright of all the bad in the world, and the panic of getting everything done in time.

2. If I live my life driven by love, I am determined, single-minded, and obsessed with feeling affection for others, liking others, adoring life, worshipping a higher power, being devoted to good, and caring for others.

Looking at the two options that we are all faced with; it is very easy to see which is the better of the two. Yet most choose fear, as I did for many years.

After looking at the grim and negative way a life driven by fear will affect us, how is it possible that we choose to keep living that way? I think it has to do with many variables, but the one thing that I want to drive home here is that it is a choice just like every other choice we make in life. Until I was able to swallow that little pill of truth, there was nothing I could do about living my life driven by fear. You see, until I can assume responsibility for living such a miserable life, I can do nothing about it because, if it is all the fault of my parents, my wife, the war, the job, my boss, and so on, I am screwed because I cannot change them. The good news is that I can change myself and choose differently.

So if fear ought to be classified as stealing, what does it steal from us? I think a very long list is in order at this point. Fear often makes us too scared to do the following:

- Ask that special person to prom because she might say no
- Try out for the football team because someone told me I was too small
- Apply to the college I really wanted to go to because my parents would not approve
- Apply for that job because I was not good enough
- Ask someone to marry me because I couldn't deal with the possibility of rejection
- Have kids because I might suck as a parent
- Move across the country because I may not like the people there
- Take the next promotion because I might not be as good as my bosses thought I was
- Change careers in midlife because my plan might fail
- Take a dream vacation to the islands because the plane might crash
- Ask for help from another because he might think I am weak
- Dance at the party because others might laugh at me
- Write a book because no one may like it
- Follow my passion in life because everyone said that it was too risky and that I should stick with what I was good at

- Succeed because there would be big expectations on me to perform
- Say no because others might think I am scared

This is a list of questions that belongs to the "what if" types of the world—you know, the ones who are always asking, "What if this doesn't work?" or "What if you fail?"

The question that I now propose to those who live life asking those questions is this: "What if it all works out perfectly?" Many of them will not entertain my questions because that would force them to look at the possibility of being wrong. You see, it is very easy to live life in fear, but the irony is that it is painful. Easy is usually connected to something good but not so in this case. This explains why so many choose to live in fear. It is easy! Living in love is not easy. Walking a faith-based life is not easy. Walking with courage through fear is scary ... until you do it! So that's it—Nike got it right years ago: "Just do it."

As simple as that short statement may sound, it is simply perfect because all that is required on my part is taking action. I have to stop philosophizing about doing things and taking risks because empty, hollow words do not provide the necessary work required to make decisions and take actions.

So how did I move from a life driven by fear into a life driven by love? The answer is one simple word—faith.

Until I was willing to believe that there was something bigger than me and bigger than all of you, everything I had or felt was dependent on me, and dependent on you. You and I are humans and will fail at some point, so as long as all my eggs are in this basket, I have good reason to believe that many will be broken. I have justifiable fear, which is crippling.

I had to become willing to believe, to figure out what it was that I did believe, to make a decision to act as if this belief was a truth, and then take action to test the hypothesis of faith. I had to do that same thing over and over again, and in time I no longer had to act "as if" because the successes of this process far outweighed the perceived failures. I say *perceived failures* because, looking back, I see that they were not failures; they were just a part of my story and one that had to play out in order to get to where I am now. I can look back at my decisions and actions that worked out in the past and could then draw strength from those successes, knowing that everything that was happening around me was not a coincidence, not happenstance, and not dumb luck. It was nothing less than faith-based decisions followed by actions with expectations of huge success on the outcome because, you see, when I believe that all that is happening is in perfect order according to my faith, the outcome is perfect every time. I didn't say I liked it every time; I said it was perfect every time, therefore successful.

One of the key differences between a person who lives in faith and one who lives in fear is this: one person has life happening around her, and the other person has life happening to her, which makes one person an observer and the other person a victim. The choice is yours, and it is one that has to be made on a daily basis. My hope for you is a life of faith because the life of a victim is not a pleasant one.

Perspective

**Viewpoint/Standpoint/Outlook/Point of
View/View/Perception/Side/Angle**
*"We are all crazy, separated only by varying
degrees of relativity and individual perspective"*
Scott Kocor

The ability to understand and embrace the full meaning and
gravity of this little word, *perspective*, is the difference between
joy and misery, understanding and fighting, sympathy and cruelty,
love and hate, right and wrong, and any other combination of
diametrically opposing emotions or outcomes.

Let me be the first to tell you that I screw this one up just as
much if not more than the rest, but I am getting better at it. We
often hear the saying that perspective is reality, and if there ever
was a saying that was literally true, it is this one. The fact—not the
possibility or potential or assumption, but the fact—that all people
in the world get to choose their current realities that are based on

their perceptions of their current situations is something we need to understand to our core. Stop and think about that. According to "them," they are right at all times! So where does that leave you and me? Well, it leaves us with our own perspectives.

Anytime I get emotional about a subject, I render myself incapable of seeing another perspective, and for a guy as passionate and outspoken as I am, this is a common occurrence. Once I have the ability to relax; take out the emotion; look at the cold, hard facts; and place myself in the other person's shoes, I can then speak the type of language required to generate forward movement in the situation, deal, or issue so that the outcome of the situation will be reached in a mature manner.

When I lose sight of the fact that perception is reality, I say things like, "I can't believe he did that," or "I cannot believe that he was so stubborn," or "What was she thinking?"

People do outlandish, crazy things all of the time. They have issues and theories and comments that make no sense to me, and you know what? They don't care. They are no different than me. They have a set of rules that they live by, which formed as a result of their cultures, geographical locations, upbringings, religions, interactions with people, goals, and life experiences, just like you and me.

Perspective is not just a theory or a concrete concept; it is an ever-changing, constantly morphing, emotional process that can and will change in the blink of an eye. So why am I so surprised when someone tells me one thing this week and something different the next? I shouldn't be surprised, because much has happened to change that person's perspective in the last seven days.

Simply put, if I don't agree with someone's perspective (reality), that is my problem, not his. And if I want him to have a different reality, I have to be ready to take the actions required to change his perspective or choose to separate from him. My choice!

Chapter Nineteen

No Back-Up Plan

When I walked away from a seventeen-year career in the military, just three short years from getting a full retirement plan, I was called many things: crazy, stupid, irresponsible—but mostly stupid. I had been recruited by a start-up company to play a large role in its growth plan. I will never forget the day when my wife asked me, "So if this company doesn't work out, what is our backup plan"? My instant reply was, "There is no backup plan."

The look on her face was one of disbelief and concern, but I knew that she needed the truth. You see, I knew things were not always going to be a bed of roses as I trudged the road of an infant entrepreneur, and I knew that if I had a "fail-safe" backup plan in place, when times got hard I would quit and start following the backup plan. This mind-set was not an option for me, and it never will be. Things ended up not working out with that company, and when that day came, I did not have a backup plan. But I quickly developed a new plan.

In my experience, the only way you will ever be truly successful at anything is to become 100 percent committed to the success of that goal. If you give anything less, you will bail out when times get tough. You want to know how I know that you will bail out? Because that is what I used to do, and we are all wired the same. We like safety, security, comfort, and knowns. Most of us avoid change or risk.

Seth Godin wrote a book titled *The Dip* that I strongly suggest you read before you decide to commit to a new endeavor. Godin describes in great detail all of the reasons that a backup plan is not an option. Another great takeaway is a liberating concept that we never talk about, which is knowing when to quit something that you have started. I mean, who ever told me that there were times in life that the best and right thing to do was to quit? No one, until I read Godin's book. Knowing when to quit is just as important as knowing when to gut it out, and I now approach life looking at quitting as a strategic move, not as evidence that I'm a "quitter."

I will always have a well-thought-out plan for whatever it is I am doing or plan on doing (and I suggest you do the same), but a backup plan will not be on the table. Only when failure is not an option will I walk through the fire to reach the other side.

Chapter Twenty

Getting Comfortable
Feeling Uncomfortable

E very single thing I have talked about to this point has a common side effect: making things temporarily uncomfortable. The key word being temporarily.

My brother and I have an executive consulting company that specializes in many aspects of leadership and teamwork, and we have found that the ability to consistently perform at fluctuating levels of discomfort separates the successful leaders from the crowd. I have come to realize that the same applies to life in general.

So the fact is that none of us like to be uncomfortable. We are all creatures of habit and most times will do everything within our power to maintain the status quo to avoid the known pains and discomfort that facing our problems often produces.

Notice that I did not say that the uncomfortable feelings would be gone; I said that we have to become comfortable with feeling uncomfortable.

First of all, we have to get to the root of this discomfort, and in my opinion it is nothing more than fear. Our brains tell us that if we deal with this certain person or issue, it will only lead to more pain or change that will require more work on our part. My favorite reasoning goes something like, "If I say this, she will say that, and I will get mad, and she will probably yell, and I will yell back … blah blah blah." You know the story. The thing is that this outlandish foreshadowing is nothing more than telling myself a lie in order to avoid some mild discomfort. That's right—*mild* discomfort. The actual act of doing the task is never as bad as I make myself believe it will be.

So how, then, do I become comfortable with all of this? First of all, I have to face the core issue, and that is that I am scared. So I will ask myself this simple question: "What are you afraid of?" I can then come at the problem from a fact-finding perspective rather than an emotional basket case one. There are three questions I ask myself to help decide what to do: What is the worst that could happen? What is the best that could happen? Am I willing to do nothing and continue to suffer the consequences of doing nothing? The last question is the most important one for me.

Now for the capper! The only way to become comfortable "feeling" uncomfortable is to do the things that cause this discomfort as often as possible. What happens is that I begin to reap the benefits of having that hard conversation with my kids or boss, telling my coworkers they need to get it together, talking to my spouse about my feelings, going to that job interview, removing toxic people from my life, and so on. Once my brain has to go through the turmoil of taking these actions and feels the freedom on the other side, it (my brain) will then begin to associate these situations with positive feelings and the fear will lessen with each situation that I go through. This is a process, and for me it took years, but the only way to master it is to do it. None of us can talk or wish away problems, and change does not occur without action on our part. I must face these uncomfortable situations in every area of my life, or I will suffer the consequences of cowardice, which is by definition: weakness, fearfulness, fear or spineless. No thanks to all, I'll take the temporary discomfort of dealing with the problem!

Chapter Twenty-One

Growing = Outgrowing Others, Nothing Personal

The process of growth as an individual brings about change. This change can be very subtle and happen over years, or it can be very drastic and happen in a moment of clarity, but growth brings change one way or another. We all grow at different rates, and we all have different ways that we deal with this change.

For many years, I did everything in my power to stay the same. In fact, I thought that life was meant to be lived that way. You were supposed to take a stance on everything, and you were supposed to defend this way of life, to the death, if required. In living that way, people often faded out of my life. At the time, I thought it was cruel and unnecessary for these people to leave my life. They were my friends, my coworkers, and even my family. How could they be in perfect sync with me one day and gone the next? How could they just up and move away for some stupid job? How could they talk to that person I hate when they know I can't stand him? These are the questions of a person who has life happening to her instead of around her. The simple truth is that they were growing, which meant they were changing, and moreover, they were doing what was right for them.

Once I hit a point in my life when the old way of living was not working anymore, I decided that it was time for some growth on my part. I became hungry for more or different concepts, theories, and knowledge. I spent time with people whom I swore I would never associate with, I read books about concepts and theories that I swore I would never believe in, and I began to find answers to the questions that had baffled me my entire life. The by-product of all of this action was growth, and the direct by-product of growth is change. I became the person to whom others were saying, "What has happened to you?" "I can't believe you're not at the bars." "I can't believe you're getting out of the army." "Why don't you call anymore?" and "What do you mean you're moving?"

The point is that *when we grow, we go*! We go new places, we get new jobs, we find new friends, we get new hobbies, we stop doing old things, and we start doing new things, and in the process we move away from some of what used to be the mainstays of our lives. What I have come to realize is that this is how it is supposed to be and a very positive thing.

It is not mean, it is not wrong, and it is definitely not selfish, as many would have you to believe. It is simple cause and effect.

The people who are constants in my life are the ones who support me no matter what. The ones who complained about my growth are no longer with me but are welcome back anytime they choose to play a positive role in my life. It is not up to me to make or expect anyone to grow at the same pace that I grow, and it is not up to me to help them see my point of view on why I think they should change. It is up to me to take care of me, and if that means that the changes I am going through pull me into places others don't want to go, so be it. Desired change and personal growth in one person can only be viewed as negative from the perspectives of those who care only for themselves, and they make up this crowd of those who are being outgrown. It's nothing personal—just facts.

Chapter Twenty-Two

Making the Rules Up As You Go

As a child, I never liked to play games with kids who were always making up the rules of a game as they went along. This type of behavior almost always meant that I would end up losing, which tended to piss me off.

As an adult, I applied the same point of view to those who seemed to be making up the rules as they went along. The problem with this mind-set is that I was no longer on the playground. I was in the real world.

The previous chapters are full of the guidelines I use to make up my rules. That being said, it is obvious that there is absolutely no way these rules will maintain consistency.

Once again, this is not meant to be applied to every aspect of my life, nor is it a free pass to change the rules without first considering the consequences for those who will be affected.

What it does mean is that the rules I used when I was twenty-one probably will not work well at thirty-seven. People in my life at age thirty-seven who are still using the rules of a twenty-one-year-old may view my new rules as stringent and may have an opinion about the way I view the world under my new rules. That is their issue and not mine.

When I read a new piece of information or hear a great concept or truth that is profound to me, it is probable that this newfound perspective will push me to make a change. And when I decide to make a change or adjustment to the rules that I apply to the world and myself, I will always end up being questioned by those who know me best. They will say things like, "You never told me that," "That goes against everything you have ever said," "That is the dumbest thing I have ever heard," or "You can't just make up the rules as you go." But guess what—I *can* make up the rules as I go because I know that I am no longer on the elementary school playground. I am an individual who has chosen to grow up, and in doing so, I make my own decisions and rules, as should you.

Are there any "rules" that you have in your life that are no longer working for you? If so, why not change them? The question that I ask of those in your situation, or of myself in regards to this subject it this "Why do you do it that way?" If the answer is, "Because that is the way I have always done it", then it is definitely time to change the rules, because that is not a valid reason and does not describe the oh so important "why" that we need to understand, in order to make sense of life. Ask the simple question of why you still do the same things and make changes as your answers suggest them.

Chapter Twenty-Three

Life Situations Are Temporary

For many years of my life, not only did life happen *to* me, it was if each new set of circumstances was going to *last a lifetime.* With each new turn of events, my spirits would rise and fall, spike and plummet, beginning an amazing roller-coaster ride of life-changing circumstances filled with rash decisions and followed by undesirable consequences and regret.

When things were great, I acted as if they were never going to change, and when things were bad, I acted as if life would soon be over, neither of which were true.

What I have learned is that things are nothing more than what they are, and they are only as good or bad as my perception makes them out to be. Fully understanding that everything is temporary is a bit disheartening when I apply it to the good times, but what a huge relief to have this clarity during the bad times.

I think that the reason that we are always told that "time heals all wounds" is because it is only in the by-product that time produces, which we are afforded the gift of hindsight, and with this gift comes a new truth, our present truth, which is that the so called bad experience that we had was actually the perfect catalyst to thrust us in the direction of our current reality, which we absolutely love, which in turn made the so called bad experience a great experience that we should not have complained about so much in the first place. This is a truth that I must do my best to remember, for in it lies one of grandest secrets to a pleasant life.

Chapter Twenty-Four

Being Comfortable All Alone, Still and Silent

Doesn't the word *comfortable* sum up what we are striving for on a daily basis, in all that we do? I think so. We want to make enough money to become comfortable. We adjust our position in a seat to become more comfortable. We work out so we will be more comfortable with the way we look at our twentieth reunion. We have a few drinks to be more comfortable on the blind date. We will do almost anything to become more comfortable!

So why is this comfort that we seek so elusive? For me, it is because I seek comfort in all the wrong places and in all the wrong ways. For many years of my life, the worst possible circumstance that I could be in was to be in a quiet room all by myself—no radio, no TV, no book to read, just my thoughts and me. This was absolute torture and a situation I avoided at all costs. Why? I couldn't stand myself.

I could not stand to be alone with my thoughts because my thoughts were filled with regret, shame, guilt, fear, worry, panic, anxiety, and the rest of the terrors that many of us live with. I had to find a way to take the focus off of what it was I despised (me), so I surrounded myself with people and stuff. I had tons of "friends." I was the guy who knew everyone and always, and I mean always, had something going on. If there wasn't a party, I threw one. If you were in your room enjoying some peace and quiet while reading a book, I was the guy who showed up and *forced* you to hang out, have a beer, or go to a club. I did anything to get away from myself.

I bring all of this up because I know that I was not and am not the only one who suffers from this affliction of being restless, irritable, and discontent with life. I know this because I see it everywhere and from so many who still suffer. It really sucks to live in such a state of existence, and I am here to tell you that you don't have to. Believe it or not, it is a choice.

The ability to become comfortable all alone, still and silent, is nothing short of a gift. This gift is yours for the taking, but it comes at a price: the willingness and determination to live in a fashion that I have talked about in all of the previous chapters. There is no great secret known by the yogis of India that allows only them to be able to meditate in silence at peace and ease. There are no great prayers you have to pray, no white-light moments required. You are no different than me, and I know that this state of being content is possible because I have it in my life today.

The days of being alone with my thoughts in a state of panic are a thing of the past. In fact, I absolutely love time by myself. This is nothing short of a miracle. Now let me throw out an itty-bitty disclaimer: I do not live a life of pure Zen. Shocker, I know!

I am married, have two active kids, and am a business owner. Therefore, I have my moments of insanity, but they are the exception, not the rule. And as I continue to grow and make better decisions, the period of time between the insanity outbreaks increases substantially.

The key to my success in finding this inner peace was simple and yet the hardest thing I have ever done. I had to do the following:

- Admit that I didn't have nor would I ever have all the answers
- Admit I was powerless over everything except my thoughts
- Develop a relationship with a God that I understood and trusted
- Do my best to clean up the messes I had made in the past
- Quit making the same mistakes
- Learn to love myself first

Chapter Twenty-Five

My Journey, My God

None of what I am about to say is meant to be negative or judgmental about any faith or religion. Every person has a right and a personal reason to believe in a brand of religion or God that they have come to know, trust, and have faith in, and I respect that right and their reasons. I am choosing to share a part of my life story with you with respect to my faith. This is very personal and something that I contemplated not writing about. I did not want to offend or stir up controversy. I did not want to possibly have folks not read this book if they found out that I believed in a manner that was not in alignment with their faith, but tonight, after I lay down in bed with my wife, I couldn't go to sleep. I felt compelled to get up and work on this book. I started off with a new chapter, but the words would not come, so I sat staring at the blank page—and it came to me that I needed to share my story of faith with you. So here goes.

I was raised in a Christian home and attended Sunday school and church on a regular basis. I never did feel comfortable in either place, not because the people there were wrong or bad and not because I was wrong or bad; it was just the way I felt. I cannot say that I really contemplated why I felt uncomfortable; I just assumed that that was the way that everyone felt at that age. All I wanted to do from the moment I got to church was to get out as fast as possible. This feeling never left me over the years of my adolescence. Once I had moved away from home, I chose not to attend church.

During the years after leaving home and joining the military, I often contemplated God but never did understand Him, or Her, or whatever "It" was all about. There were a few things that I definitely knew: there was a God, I was a sinner, and I was more than likely going to hell. That was the baggage I carried for quite a few years.

I won't belabor the low point of my life other than to say that it was not pleasant, filled with booze, drugs, promiscuous sex, and anything else I could get my hands on to fill the void in my life, a void that was the size of a Mack truck. I ran on self-will alone and took all that I could from the world until I finally hit bottom. I finally surrendered, and in this surrender, I was able to seek the knowledge that I needed to have a relationship with a God that I had never been told about.

The key word to everything I just said is *relationship*—not affair; not one-night stand; not on again, off again, but a relationship. This word carries with it a hell of a lot of work. All relationships require certain things: attention, dialogue, affection, love, and commitment. There are no days off in a serious relationship. This communion that I have with my God is one that requires daily effort and maintenance, and that's something that I think is worth pointing out. Now back to my story.

Early on in my journey with God, I had to keep things simple. I had to come to understand something that was very hard to believe: God loved me no matter what, and all of my mistakes and poor decisions and the hurt I had caused meant nothing to this God. This God was not going to ever punish me or judge me. In a nutshell,

I was told to come up with what my own personal God would be, and I did, and there started my journey with my God.

I was dedicated to having a relationship with this God, which meant daily prayer and meditation, prayers for strength in the morning, talks throughout the day, and prayers of thanks at night. I was told that God did not mind if I could not pray the way I had heard preachers pray; in fact, God did not care what I said when I prayed. I began to have conversations with God, to drive with the radio off and just talk to God. The examples could continue for the next twenty pages, but I think you get the point. I had found a God that was different from anything that I had ever been told about, and I had something special—so special, in fact, that it changed my life completely. This went on very smoothly for about the next seven years, and then a new question came to me: What exactly do I believe? I set out to answer this question no matter the work required.

This new journey was started primarily because I did not know what to tell my children. They would ask why we didn't go to church, for which I had no good answer. In fact, at the time, if someone asked what I believed, I would immediately say I was a Christian. I mean, I was raised a Christian, I was baptized, and as a kid I had seven years of perfect attendance at Sunday school. I had to be a Christian as far as I knew, but I was not sure anymore, and I believed that I owed an answer to my children and, more so, to myself.

My search began by reading many books on many topics. I took an interest in reading about religions. I had conversations until three o'clock in the morning with anyone who had a profound belief in anything. I wanted to know what they believed and why they believed it. I wanted to know why they thought their brand of religion or belief system was right; moreover, I wanted to know why they thought everyone else was wrong.

You see, it was all very confusing for me. In one breath, these people would speak of a God who was loving and compassionate and the next moment, they talked about a God who was judgmental and condemning—so much so that He or She would throw you into eternal hell for doing some things or for not doing others. This was a God who kept score and took care of some but banished others, and every person I spoke to had his or her own way of interpreting information. There was very little consistency, which was confusing as well.

About a year into this journey, I definitely knew what I didn't believe in but was still unsure about what I did believe in. I'll never forget the look on my wife's face when I told her that I had realized that I had been walking around for years lying to people by telling them I was a Christian because I was not a Christian. She thought I had lost my mind, but little did she know that I was actually on the road to finding it.

One day, I was having a very heated debate with a group of Christian men. My question to them was a scenario-based one that was something to this effect: "If I am in a room with a Jew, a Muslim, a Buddhist monk, a scientologist, and a child-molesting rapist; we all know that death is coming in one minute; we are asked if we would accept Jesus Christ as our only Lord and Savior; and the child molester agrees but the rest do not, is the child molester the only one going to heaven?" Their answer was yes, that was correct. This was not something I could believe then, nor do I believe it now. I refuse to believe that some are saved and all others are screwed.

What I will tell you next was the turning point in figuring out what I do believe.

During the process of transitioning out of the army in 2009, I went to a store to look for a card for my wife, and in this process I saw a quote on a card that said, "Life begins at the end of your comfort zone." The quote is from Neale Donald Walsch, from his

Conversations with God series of books. I had no idea who Neale was, nor had I read any of his books, but when I saw that quote, I knew it to be true. I was personally in the middle of beginning a new life that was well outside of my comfort zone. So when I set up my e-mail signature block with my new company, I included that quote and Neale's name under my own. Now for the rest of the story.

A bit later, I was with my wife at a Borders bookstore that was going out of business, and we were just killing some time, looking for some good deals, when I looked up and saw the name Neale Donald Walsch on the spine of a book. I figured, *What the heck? I have had this guy's quote in my e-mail for the last twelve months. I'll see what his book is called.* The name of the book was *Happier than God.* I laughed when I it and said to myself, "This is nontraditional blasphemy, which is right up my alley!"

The following evening, I was leaving for a business trip to New Mexico, so I decided to buy the book to read during the flight. By the time I landed in Albuquerque the following night, I knew I had finally read what I had always thought and felt. It was an earth-shaking event for me. I immediately called my wife and asked her to go back to the bookstore to see if they had *Conversations with God*, also by Walsch, and they did. When I got home from my trip, I dove into the new *Conversations with God* trilogy and was even more amazed. Up to that point, I had read books about the law of attraction, about quantum physics, and about energy, frequencies, and levels that each travel; intention; manifesting; and all the rest, but I had never read a book or talked to anyone who could put into words what I had known and felt all along. But it had finally happened, and there was no doubt in my mind that I had attracted this new knowledge and insight into my life.

At this point, I want to do my best to answer a question that you may have: "So who do you follow or look to for spiritual guidance?" I am not a follower of any one person, any one faith, or any one idea.

I have a handful of teachers whom I believe are here to help folks like me—you know, the ones who never did get the God thing from a "traditional source." Walsch managed to speak to me in very plain and common terms, and in doing so, he said the same thing that many others have said, only differently. All of the teachers, such as Wayne Dyer, Deepak Chopra, Walsch, and all the rest, are just messengers as far as I am concerned, and they happen to speak to my brand of spirituality. For you, it may be different. Either way, I hope you never stop looking until you have the great *aha* moment in life.

So what do I believe? I believe that God lives inside of us all and that God speaks to us all. I mean, if God spoke to the prophets two thousand years ago, is there any reason that He, She, or It would not do the same today? I can't come up with any reasons why not. I choose to believe that God speaks to me in many different ways and as often as I am truly listening. Some call it their gut feeling or the like, but I believe that it is nothing less than communication from an all-powerful guiding force. I also decided to believe that God is in me, and therefore with me, always, and with this belief comes the comfort of never needing God, for how can I need something that is part of me?

I believe that God is energy, that solid forms of energy are matter, and that we are all made of the same matter. Therefore, I believe that we are all one. Because I believe this, I know that to do good for one is to do good for all, and to do harm to one is to do harm to all, myself included. I choose to believe that there is no hell other than that which we create here on earth through poor decisions and actions. I choose to believe that life is not a destination but a journey that was meant to be full of experiences that can be produced only by faith, for without faith, fear will hamper the ability to experience the wonderment of life. I choose to believe that there is more than enough for all of us. I choose to believe that since I have God in me, I can manifest into my life anything that I hold in the most secret of places, my mind. I choose to believe that life is eternal. I also know this: I will continue to seek, listen, read, and learn, and in this process, I feel certain that how I view my God at present will not be the same way I view God a year or two from now. But that is irrelevant as long as the core relationship is present and active. I believe that there were, are, and will be prophets and enlightened souls here on earth to provide guidance to those who listen. I believe that all religions worship the same God. In closing, I believe that God wants for me what I want for me; if not, why did She give me the ability to choose? By the way, I do not think God is a She, nor do I think God is a He or an It. I believe that God is God and makes up each and every thing there is, was, and will be. I use the word *She* often to remind myself to stay open-minded.

What you choose to believe is up to you and you alone. I am responsible only for my relationship with my God. If the belief you have now or that you have been taught isn't working for you or you have "hard" questions about certain things that have never been fully answered, I urge you to seek the answers for yourself and find your own truth—no one else's.

Our beautiful family

Daily Routines that Change My Life

Each morning, I wake up to the beginning of an eternal moment that will be in perfect harmony with my choices. Some choices come with consequences that I perceive to be good, and some come with consequences that I perceive to be bad. I want to share with you the choices that I do my best to make and the actions that I perform as a daily routine to help keep me centered and sane.

- Pray or meditate for a minimum of five minutes before I get out of bed
- Write or type a gratitude list
- Make a journal entry
- Do some type of physical activity

The total time required to pull off these actions is about an hour. I do all of them only on days that I want to have a great day. Give it a try for ten days in a row. What do you have to lose?

The love of my life... best friend and the most beautiful woman in the world, my wife Stacy, and me.

"Your Life" Parting Thoughts

I wish you the best of luck and unwavering faith in taking and maintaining responsibility for your life. It is my hope that you will never settle for anything less than what it is you are capable of achieving in your life, which in my opinion is anything. Let no one and no thing, steal from you what it is you were born to become or achieve. Looking forward!

S.D.S.
Please e mail me any thoughts or questions
scotdspooner@yourlife2012.com

Follow "Your Life" on Facebook
https://www.facebook.com/pages/Your-Life-By-Scot-D-Spooner/190428714374290

My lifelong hero, business partner, and
brother, Tom Spooner, and me

Labyrinth Guides

http://www.labyrinthgc.com

Our leadership and team-building company

http://www.invictusagi.com

Our tactical training and consulting company

About the Author

Scot has a self-appointed PhD on the subject of life.

Scot believes that his life of perceived struggle and unfortunate circumstances are the rule in today's society, not the exception. Scot says, "I am the average American who has suffered the common problems of the world at large, but what makes me different is how I ended up after going through these problems." Scot believes that there is hope for all who choose to take responsibility for their lives' present circumstances and get into action, which is what this book is focused on.

Scot is a seventeen-year veteran of the US Army, fourteen of which were spent as a Green Beret assigned to Third Special Forces Group and First Special Forces Operational Detachment Delta.

Scot is a husband of 13 years, a father of two beautiful children, and a courageous and successful author and entrepreneur.

Scot is the cofounder and managing partner of S&T Incorporated, parent company of Labyrinth Guides Consulting www.labyrinthgc. com and Invictus Alliance Group www.invictusagi.com.

Scot is thirty-seven years old and lives with his beautiful family in Cary, North Carolina.